"60" Seconds

Inspirational Minutes

Carol Dixon

WESTBOW
PRESS
A DIVISION OF THOMAS NELSON

WestBow Press books may be ordered through booksellers or by contacting:
WestBow Press
A Division of Thomas Nelson
1663 Liberty Drive
Bloomington, IN 47403
www.westbowpress.com
1-(866) 928-1240

Because of the dynamic nature of the Internet, any web addresses or links contained
in this book may have changed since publication and may no longer be valid.

The views expressed in this work are solely those of the author and do not necessarily reflect
the views of the publisher, and the publisher hereby disclaims any responsibility for them.

Any people depicted in stock imagery provided by Thinkstock are models,
and such images are being used for illustrative purposes only.

Certain stock imagery © Thinkstock.

ISBN: 978-1-4497-6441-8 (sc)
ISBN: 978-1-4497-6440-1 (e)
Library of Congress Control Number: 2012915544

Printed in the United States of America

WestBow Press rev. date: 09/27/2012

DEDICATION

This book is dedicated to my children and their spouses: Rick and Valerie, Tasha and Charod, and my youngest son, Harley.

To my grandchildren: Rick II, D'Mitri, Jeremy, Conor, and my only granddaughter, Rheya.

To my siblings and their spouses: Harley (1942-2011) and Vernette, Lillian, Quanita and Ethman, Johnette and James.

I can't tell you often enough how very proud I am of all of you. Your constant example of faith, love, and dedication to the LORD and to His people brings honor, joy, and purpose to my life.

And to my KAINOS Church Family, your love, loyalty, support, and enthusiasm are second to none. Our greatest days are ahead!!!

I Love You All

"CHOOSE LIFE"

CHOOSE LIFE

***

*C*hoose this day to serve God.

To hear, obey and to move in Him.

The scripture says we have a choice to live or die…to be blessed or cursed…to serve God not to serve Him.

God wants us to enjoy the good life He made possible for us, but we are the ones who must make the choice.

There is power in choice. God won't make us do anything.

The responsibility for the direction of your life is in your hands.

It is your choices and decisions, not your circumstances that create the quality of your life.

You need to understand that you are where you are today because of the choices and decisions you made yesterday.

Choose to hear, obey and move in God; make a quality decision to serve Him today.

Choose to enjoy the abundant life God's provided for you.

"Trust me" you will be glad that you did!

Deuteronomy 30:19 – I AM Carol Dixon!!!

DEUTERONOMY 30:19
*I call heaven and earth to record this day against you, [that]
I have set before you life and death, blessing and cursing:
therefore choose life that both thou and thy seed may live:*

"A NEW LIFE IN CHRIST"

✦❀✦

When we receive Jesus, we are born again.

We experience the new birth when the seed of
God's Word is planted in our spirit.

The incorruptible Word of God puts a light on the inside of you.

Your light attracts others to you because God, who is the "light",
dwells in you, and that light produces a "new life" in you.

It was not passed on to you by your parents, for
the life they gave you will fade away.

This new one will last forever, for it comes from Christ.

That new life can be yours beginning right now.

For it is by believing in your heart, and with
your mouth tell others of your faith.

Turn away from the past and press forward to the good
plan that God have had for you from the beginning.

Then the light of God will help you to live your life in such a
way that you may draw others into the Kingdom of God!

1Peter 1:23 – I AM Carol Dixon!!!

1 PETER 1:23
*Being born again, not of corruptible seed, but of incorruptible,
by the Word of God, which liveth and abideth for ever.*

"GOD'S WORD IS NOURISHMENT"

❧❖❧

*O*nce you decide to give your heart to Jesus, you need to trust Him every day in every way, and you will find out that God's favor and protection will just begin to happen in your life, and when they do, don't act as though they didn't.

Give God praise and glory for every little blessing – from finding a good parking space to receiving an unexpected financial gift.

Let your roots grow down into Him then nourish your roots by studying the Word of God and listening to His Word being preached.

Faith comes by hearing – and hearing – and hearing.

Even if you think you've heard it all before, you'll learn something new that will strengthen your walk with the Lord.

"Get Rooted" and you will find yourself praising God in every situation and over every circumstance because you are rooted and built up in Him.

Colossians 2:6, 7 – I AM Carol Dixon!!!

COLOSSIANS 2:6 & 7

6V As ye have therefore received Christ Jesus the Lord, [so] walk ye in Him:

7V Rooted and built up in Him, and stablished in the faith, as ye have been taught, abounding therein with thanksgiving.

"YOUR GUIDE & INSTRUCTOR"

The Word of God is so strong and powerful.

When it is planted down deep in your heart, it will help you
in times of discouragement and minister joy to your heart.

I like the idea that God has promised to watch out for
the pathway of life that is best suited for me.

And I love the instructions of the Bible – God's instruction book.

Why?

Because they promise to guide and direct my paths
toward the very best that He has for me.

That's what I want, especially in these times. Further,
God promises to observe my progress.

He means if I take a wrong turn, I'll feel a little nudge in my
heart, and He'll tell me to go in a different direction.

We can trust God, He has always given me good
advice, and He'll do the same for you.

He will keep you on the right path, and not let you
veer off in a direction where you should not go.

Thank You Lord for Your guidance and instruction.

Psalm 32:8 – I AM Carol Dixon!!!

PSALM 32:8
*I will instruct thee and teach thee in the way which
thou shalt go: I will guide thee with Mine eye.*

Carol Dixon   4   "60 Seconds"

"ACQUAINT YOURSELF WITH GOD"

❦

*D*o you realize that in this day and age, the only way you can have peace is to be acquainted with God?

People who are acquainted with "Almighty God" don't react to trouble the same way as those who have never had a relationship with Him.

Those of us who are acquainted with our heavenly Father know the secret to letting go of things we cannot change.

We have learned to let God in and give Him charge of our lives, our situations, our challenges, and our circumstances.

Take a moment today to get quiet and listen.

If you and God have grown apart, I believe your effort to become reacquainted with Him will result in God speaking to you in the midst of your deepest troubles.

Stay acquainted with Him, and the next time trouble knocks at your door, you can open it with confidence in God.

Job 22:21 – I AM Carol Dixon!!!

JOB 22:21
Acquaint now thyself with Him, and be at peace:
thereby good shall come unto thee.

"BE A SOLIDER IN GOD'S ARMY"

*A*re you aware that you are a soldier in the army of the Lord?

You weren't drafted – you enlisted in the army of God when you made a decision to accept Jesus Christ as your Lord and Savior.

As a young recruit, you must train spiritually for spiritual warfare.

Why?

So you'll be prepared for battle – because battles come to all of us!

Spiritual training includes reading and studying the Word of God, attending a good bible–teaching church, participating in bible studies, prayer groups, and outreaches that touch your community.

Good training will help you when you need it
most to win the battles you face in life.

These battles are sometimes long and difficult to
deal with, but ultimately, you will win.

Desire to be a first class soldier and be fit for the battle.

Because with God as your commander in chief, you win!

2 Timothy 2:4 – I AM Carol Dixon!!!

2 TIMOTHY 2:4
*No man that warreth entangleth himself with the affairs of [this] life;
that he may please Him who hath chosen him to be a soldier.*

"GOD'S STRENGTH AND PROTECTION"

᠆✦᠆

*I*f there was ever a time when we needed strength and protection wherever we go, it is now.

In a day when sin and its dangerous effects are everywhere, it is comforting to find in God's Word that He provides strength and protection wherever we go!

When you're out running errands or accomplishing certain goals today, keep in mind that God will fill you with all the strength you need to accomplish whatever it is He's called you to do today, and He'll give you protection wherever you go if your trust is in Him.

Just knowing this can cause today to be a wonderful day for you!

Pray this prayer with me: "God, I thank You that I have Your protection wherever I go, and Your strength for whatever I need to do today.

How blessed I am to have You walking beside me.

You are my strength and protection, Amen."
Psalm 18:32 – I AM Carol Dixon!!!

PSALM 18:32

[It is] God that girdeth me with strength, and maketh my way perfect.

"GO FORWARD, AND NOT BACKWARD"

If you want to keep going backwards instead of going forward, then according to scripture, all you have to do is to be stubborn, follow your own way and not listen to God.

If you want to go forward however, and do something lasting for Jesus, then all you have to do is obey His commands.

It seems simple, doesn't it?

It is simple the only way to live and be happy, moving forward and succeeding in life both naturally and spiritually is to simply be obedient to God.

He will never ask you to do the impossible; following His guidance will always lead to happiness.

Don't go down the road that takes you two steps forward and one step back because of disobedience.

Leave what's behind you and press forward to God's very best for your life.

Why not begin today? Go forward not backwards.

Jeremiah 7:23 & 24 - I AM Carol Dixon!!!

JEREMIAH 7:23 & 24

23v But this thing commanded I them, saying, Obey My voice, and I will be your God, and ye shall be My people: and walk ye in all the ways that I have commanded you, that it may be well unto you.

24v But they hearkened not, nor inclined their ear, but walked in the counsels [and] in the imagination of their evil heart, and went backward, and not forward.

"THE POWER OF AGREEMENT"

※◆※

*G*od always promises to answer any prayers that line up with His will in 1 John, whether we are praying alone or with someone else.

But in Matthew there is a direct quotation of Jesus.

He actually said that He gets involved - He is present in other words, and there is power in times of united prayers between two or more believers.

Is the prayer of agreement a guarantee that God will answer in the way you want Him to?

God would never grant a foolish or selfish request, but there is no question in my mind that prayers of agreement are special to God.

Find someone to pray with you – a prayer partner.

Put together your list of requests for things about which you need God's wisdom.

Prayer is simply communication with God.

Sometimes you talk while He listens, and other times He'll talk through impressions in your spirit - and you'll listen.

Don't underestimate the power of agreement!

Matthew 18:19 & 20 - I AM Carol Dixon!!!

MATTHEW 18: 19 & 20

19V Again I say unto you, That if two of you shall agree on earth as touching any thing that they shall ask, it shall be done for them of my Father which is in heaven.

20V For where two or three are gathered together in My name, there am I in the midst of them.

"WE'RE ALWAYS IN GOD'S THOUGHTS"

⋙⋘

You are always on God's mind.

There is never a time when His thoughts are not directed toward you.

And He can do things for you that nobody else can.

You can sit and look at an idol and pray to it all
day long, but it's not thinking about you.

It can't do anything for you.

It's made of china, porcelain, wood, or clay.

Why would anyone think an idol could perform miracles?

But we serve a God who can and does specialize in miracles.

Think about what you really need today.

Are you single and looking for a mate?
Are you married and having some challenges in your relationship?

Are you the parent of a teen who has decided
that following your rules is out of style?

Be assured that God can and will handle any circumstance you're facing.

God is well able to do great and glorious things for you.

He will perform miracles for you when you need them.

You are always in God's thoughts.

Psalm 40:5 - I AM Carol Dixon!!!

Carol Dixon 10 *"60 Seconds"*

PSALM 40:5

*Many, O LORD my God, [are] thy wonderful works [which]
Thou hast done, and Thy thoughts [which are] to us-ward: they
cannot be reckoned up in order unto Thee: [if] I would declare
and speak [of them], they are more than can be numbered.*

"HE'S A GREAT GOD!"

～✿～

*G*od's greatness is unsearchable.

Who can fathom the greatness of God?

His Name is to be continually praised, He's a mighty God.

He's a loving God – filled with kindness and tender mercy.

Sometime we just need to stop and tell Him how much we love and adore Him and thank Him for who He is and all He's done for us.

Praise is an important part of a successful Christian life.

God's Word, which is always right, says it is an appropriate thing to do.

If you are musically inclined you may want to sing some of the psalms out loud or play an instrument in the praise of the goodness of God.

You may just want to play music on the radio or cd.

In whatever way you decide to do it, don't ever forget to let your praise drift heavenward toward God.

Let Him know how much you appreciate Him.

Psalm 48:1 – I AM Carol Dixon!!!

PSALM 48:1
Great [is] the LORD, and greatly to be praised in the city of our God, [in] the mountain of His holiness.

"AS LONG AS YOU HAVE BREATH, PRAISE THE LORD"

If you're breathing, you ought to be praising the Lord.

It's that simple.

God has given us so much to be thankful for.
Every day He loads us with His benefits.

They are listed specifically in Psalms 103:

He forgives all your sins. He heals you. He ransoms you from hell.

He fills your life with good things, so your
youth is renewed like the eagles.

He gives justice to all who are treated unfairly.
He reveals His will and nature to you.
He is slow to get angry and full of kindness and love.

He has removed your sins as far away as the east is from the west,
and His lovingkindness is from everlasting to everlasting.

Let your heart soar today with praise to God for all He has done for you.

If you're not use to praising God, just try it this week.
I believe you'll have a better week than you've had for a
long time. Psalm 150:6 – I AM Carol Dixon!!!

PSALM 150:6
Let every thing that hath breath praise the LORD. Praise ye the LORD.

"GOD IS FAITHFUL"

⊱⊰

*H*ebrews 11 is an especially good faith – building chapter in the Bible.

Imagine God telling one hundred year old Abraham, and his wife Sarah, that they would have a son at their age.

You probably know the story – Sarah laughed.

But Abraham believed that if God said it, He was well able to do anything He promised.

Sarah later realized that God, who gave her His promise, would certainly do what He said.

Now all we have to do is take the promises of God and believe them.

It's so simple.

If God said it, you can believe it because He sure wouldn't lie to you.

So let's judge Him faithful as Abraham and Sarah did.

You may not want a child when you're one hundred years old, but He'll do other things for you when you judge Him faithful and believe that He won't go back on His Word – know that something that you want is going to happen!

Hebrews 11:1 – I AM Carol Dixon!!!

HEBREW 11:1
Now faith is the substance of things hoped for,
the evidence of things not seen.

"THE SEED IS THE WORD"

❧✦❧

God uses His Word as seed to produce a harvest.

What do you want from God?

If you want healing, look up healing seeds
(scriptures that apply to healing)!

If you want a miracle, sow some miracle seed
(scriptures that describe miracles)!

If you need deliverance from fear, habits, or satan's power, then get the
appropriate seeds (find where it is written in the Word) and sow them
in your heart, make a list of the verses that apply to your situation.

Repeat them aloud every day – or several times a day.

Plant them down deep on the inside of you.

These are the promises of God to you!

They are living seeds with divine potential to change your life.

Put God's Word in your heart and nourish it
daily with prayer and thanksgiving.

God is faithful to make it grow, and your harvest will surely come.

Luke 8:5 & 11 – I AM Carol Dixon!!!

LUKE 8:5 & 11

*5V A sower went out to sow his seed: and as he sowed, some fell by the
way side; and it was trodden down, and the fowls of the air devoured it.*

11V Now the parable is this: The seed is the Word of God.

"JESUS WILL CALM YOUR STORM"

When Jesus spoke to the sea and rebukes the wind, the raging waters settled down, all of a sudden, it was calm all around the area.

Matthew 8:27 says the disciples marveled, asking themselves what manner of Man this was that even the winds and sea obeyed Him.

This is the Man that we spend our lives talking about – the Lord Jesus Christ.

He is still available today. Most of us encounter storms in our lives at one time or another, and how comforting it is to know that the master doesn't want us to perish - that He's there to calm our storms.

I encourage you to call on Jesus when you're facing storms in your life.

He will be there to speak peace to your situation.

Nothing that you're going through is too difficult for Him.

Mark 4:37 – 39 – I AM Carol Dixon!!!

MARK 4:37-39

37V And there arose a great storm of wind, and the waves beat into the ship, so that it was now full.

38V And He was in the hinder part of the ship, asleep on a pillow: and they awake Him, and say unto Him, Master, carest thou not that we perish?

39V And He arose, and rebuked the wind, and said unto the sea, Peace, be still. And the wind ceased, and there was a great calm.

"WHOM SHALL I FEAR"

❧❀❧

*F*irst John 4 tells us that fear is a tormenting spirit.

Fear and torment are attacking multitudes of people in our world today – and it is a sign that we are living in the last days.

But the Psalmist says… "Whom shall I fear?" Fear can be overcome when we believe and know that the Lord is our light and salvation… God is our Father and He loves us.

By the power of His Word, we can be lifted out of the darkness of intense, overpowering fear and oppression.

We can make a habit of confessing the Word of God that specifically addresses the subject of fear and there are many.

Begin to praise God that you have victory over fear.

Thank Him for protecting you from torment and anxiety.

Remember that you are strong in the Lord and in the power of His might.

You are more than a conqueror through Christ Jesus!

Psalm 27:1 - I AM Carol Dixon!!!

Psalm 27:1
(A Psalm] of David.] The LORD [is] my light and my salvation; whom shall I fear? the LORD [is] the strength of my life; of whom shall I be afraid?

"LIE DOWN IN PEACE AND SLEEP"

❧❧❧

A lot of people have trouble sleeping.

People are fearful of putting their head down on a pillow at night because of all the things that are going on in their world.

But Psalm 4:8 says, we can … lie down in peace and sleep … Notice that it says "in peace" not "in pieces." "I will lie down in peace and sleep, for though I am alone, Lord, you will keep me safe." What a wonderful promise!

Sometimes it seems like we're so alone.

It's so dark at the midnight hour and the early morning, but we're never alone because the Lord, who never leaves us, will keep us safe.

If you're having trouble sleeping, remember that you're never alone.

Just put your head on the pillow and sleep in peace because God is right there with you, even as close as the very breath that you breathe.

Psalm 4:8 - I AM Carol Dixon!!!

PSALM 4:8
I will both lay me down in peace, and sleep: for thou, LORD, only makest me dwell in safety.

"WE ARE NOT WITHOUT FAITH"

❦

We know we cannot please God without faith - it's impossible.

But there's no need to worry about not having faith
because the Bible says that God has given faith to each of
us and faith will grow as we hear the Word of God.

When we take the time to hear and study the Word,
it will produce in us a steady growth of faith.

Our faith in the name of Jesus will result in beginning to see ourselves
as redeemed, healthy, whole, happy, blessed, and prosperous.

With our measure of faith, we can speak out
of the abundance of our hearts.

Jesus said that a man will bring forth good things
out of the good treasure of his heart.

Just a fraction of a measure of faith can help us refuse
to participate when the devil tempts us to sin.

Use the measure of faith that God has given you to fight the devil!

You have everything you'll ever need to be victorious!

Romans 12:3 - I AM Carol Dixon!!!

ROMANS 12:3

*For I say, through the grace given unto me, to every man
that is among you, not to think [of himself] more highly
than he ought to think; but to think soberly, according as
God hath dealt to every man the measure of faith.*

"YOU CAN HAVE GOD'S FAVOR IN A WICKED WORLD"

Throughout history, the wickedness of the world has broken God's heart.

That's how it was in Noah's day.

It was so bad that God was sorry He had even created mankind!

And today it seems even worse.

But the Bible says that even in all that wickedness, God saw Noah.

He saw that Noah was living right and raising his family in a Godly manner – and because of Noah's goodness, he found favor in the sight of the Lord.

The world may have been in a terrible mess, but God noticed that at least one man was righteous and true and He spared Noah and his family.

Our world may be in a mess today, but still there are people who are righteous and true – people who find favor in God's sight.

Rejoice that you are a child of Almighty God.

Conduct yourself in a manner that gains God's favor and do your part to make this world a better place!

Genesis 6: 5 &6 - I AM Carol Dixon!!!

GENESIS 6: 5 & 6

5V And GOD saw that the wickedness of man [was] great in the earth, and [that] every imagination of the thoughts of His heart [was] only evil continually.

6V And it repented the LORD that He had made man on the earth, and it grieved him at his heart.

Carol Dixon   20   "60 Seconds"

"THE BLESSING OF GIVING"

⚜

*G*od told Abraham that He would bless him and make him a blessing.

You cannot be a blessing until you're blessed.

God blesses those who will do what is closest to His heart – and that is: that every person on earth hears about His great love and the mercy He showed us in the death, burial, and resurrection of Jesus.

Our goal as a church has always been to spread the gospel throughout the world – to give generously in order to bless the whole world with the truth of God's Word!

God promises to bless us if we do that.

Whatever you give to God's work, He will multiply back to you.

As you continue to give, the financial seed you sow produces a harvest.

God blessed!

The lost and dying souls of the world, hear the good news and find Jesus.

Your generous giving in obedience to God makes it possible!

Genesis 12:2 - I AM Carol Dixon!!!

GENESIS 12:2
And I will make of thee a great nation, and I will bless thee, and make thy name great; and thou shalt be a blessing:

"GOD GIVES STRENGTH AND SKILLS"

I've got good news – "it's going to turn!"

Have you ever noticed how the tide of the battle turns
when we pray and ask God to get involved?

His Word promises that He'll be with us in the heat of
our battles with health, prosperity, relationships, jobs and
anything else that presents us with a challenge.

But how do you obtain strength and skills to
turn it around to work in your favor?

By knowing the Word of God, trusting in His wisdom, and
believing that God hears, understands, and desires to help you.

Search out God's promises and let Him become your immovable
rock, no matter what you're going through – when the enemy comes
against you, he has to face the rock of ages who stands with you.

Giving you the strength and skill to battle your enemies, helping
you overcome them and achieve the victory every time!

Psalm 144:1 - I AM Carol Dixon!!!

PSALM 144:1
*Blessed [be] the LORD my strength, which teacheth
my hands to war, [and] my fingers to fight:*

"YES, LORD, I'M LISTENING"

❦

I think one of the sweetest stories in the Bible is about Hannah taking her son Samuel to the tabernacle and giving him to God.

You know the story, Samuel didn't recognize the voice of God calling him and he ran to Eli, the priest, who realized that God was speaking to Samuel.

Samuel finally understood that it really was God who was trying to communicate with him, and he said, "Yes, Lord, I'm listening." God wants us to recognize when He is speaking to us.

We may not hear God talking to us audibly as Samuel did, but inside our hearts, we can hear and discern His voice.

When God calls your name and says, "I want you to do this," or "I want you to do that", hear Him in your heart and say, "yes, Lord, I'm listening," then do whatever He tells you to do!

I Samuel 1:26-28 and chapter 3:1-5 – I AM Carol Dixon!!!

1 SAMUEL 1:26 -28

26V And she said, Oh my Lord, [as] thy soul liveth, my Lord, I [am] the woman that stood by thee here, praying unto the LORD.

27V For this child I prayed; and the LORD hath given me my petition which I asked of Him:

28V Therefore also I have lent him to the LORD; as long as he liveth he shall be lent to the LORD. And he worshipped the LORD there.

1 SAMUEL 3:1-5

1V And the child Samuel ministered unto the LORD before Eli. And the Word of the LORD was precious in those days; [there was] no open vision.

2V And it came to pass at that time, when Eli [was] laid down in his place, and his eyes began to wax dim, [that] he could not see;

3V And ere the lamp of God went out in the temple of the LORD, where the ark of God [was], and Samuel was laid down [to sleep];

4V That the LORD called Samuel: and he answered, Here [am] I.

5V And he ran unto Eli, and said, Here [am] I; for thou calledst me. And he said, I called not; lie down again. And he went and lay down.

"STIRRED BY GOD'S WORD"

❧❧❧

*T*he Word of God is strong and powerful.

You need to read it, meditate on it, digest it,
walk in the light of it and confess it.

Then when trouble comes, you can be stirred
by the Word of God for yourself.

When you find out what the Word has to say and it clearly
says something about every problem, then the Word
will grow mightily in you, and you will prevail.

Perhaps you're in trouble today.

You may be dealing with sorrow and despair, but if the
Word of God is on the inside of you, you have life.

Trouble, sorrow, and despair are a part of death, but you have life
– and life always overcomes death, get stirred up on the inside.

See and feel the power of God in you, you can and will prevail.

In fact, great things are about to start happening for
you today as you are stirred by the Word!

Acts 19:20 - I AM Carol Dixon!!!

ACTS 19:20

So mightily grew the Word of God and prevailed.

"WHAT'S ON YOUR MIND?"

‿✦‿

*W*hatever your thoughts are most focused on,
will determine the direction of your life.

If your thoughts are unhealthy, ungodly and uncontrolled, they could
eventually wreck your life and possibly everyone close to you.

We all have thoughts. They are constantly there.

They control your moods, your self-image, your
lifestyle, your choices, and your destiny.

It is known as the battle between your ears.

Your thoughts are so powerful.

They can control everything in your life for either the good or the bad.

Let me ask you today – what is on your mind/ what
controls your thoughts throughout the day?

Do your thoughts line up with the Word of God?

How about your imagination?

Are your thoughts mostly good or evil?

Begin to think on God's Word.
Begin to think on what God says about you.

Think on things that are true, honest, just,
pure, lovely, and of good report.

Philippians 4:8 - I AM Carol Dixon!!!

PHILIPPIANS 4:8

Finally, brethren, whatsoever things are true, whatsoever things [are] honest, whatsoever things [are] just, whatsoever things [are] pure, whatsoever things [are] lovely, whatsoever things [are] of good report; if [there be] any virtue, and if [there be] any praise, think on these things.

"MIND GAMES"

*Have you ever tried to sleep and your mind would not shut up –
thoughts of all the things you need to do
the next day fills your mind.*

You start thinking about all kinds of things.

Your mind is a thought factory.

How do you control your mind and thoughts
instead of them controlling you?

I learned many years ago that when you say something out of your
mouth, your mind has to shut up and hear what your mouth has to say.

Try this exercise today: start counting to ten in your mind,
then, before you finish, say your name out loud.

Notice what happens to the counting in your mind-it stops!

Your mind had to shut up to hear what your mouth had to say.

Don't be a victim to mind games any longer – get control over
your mind – start confessing the Word of God out of your mouth
concerning every situation in your life and keep confessing the
Word until your mind stops thinking negative thoughts.

Your life depends on it.

Proverbs 18:21 – I AM Carol Dixon!!!

PROVERBS 18:21

*Death and life [are] in the power of the tongue: and
they that love it shall eat the fruit thereof.*

"THE POWER OF ATTRACTION"

⁓✵⁓

*D*id you know that negative imaginations will attract negative situations and positive imaginations will attract positive situations?

This is commonly referred to as the law of cause and effect.

The Bible calls it the law of sowing and reaping.

The most successful people in the world are those who have the ability to perceive what is possible even when it looks impossible.

They look beyond the obstacle blocking their success and they recognize that through perseverance, they will ultimately be victorious.

You've got to be able to see beyond your circumstances right now.

You must see God doing the impossible in your life.

Your circumstances are temporary; but God's Word is eternal.

God has good planned for you and your life.

Begin to perceive the impossible as possible in your life.

2 Corinthians 4:18 – I AM Carol Dixon!!!

2 CORINTHIANS 4:18
While we look not at the things which are seen, but at the things which are not seen: for the things which are seen [are] temporal; but the things which are not seen [are] eternal.

"A NEW MIND"

✦

When I surrendered my life to God, my life changed.

I became a new creation. However, nothing happened to my mind!

It was my spirit that was re-created.
My mind still thought like it always did.

Renewing the mind is not something that happens at
the new birth; it is a daily process that begins when you
start feeding your mind on the Word of God.

As you saturate yourself in the Word of God,
your thinking will begin to change.

"the Word of God is to dwell in our minds and in our hearts richly...".

The only way that it can dwell in you richly is by meditating on it.

Just as physical food nourishes your body, the Word
of God nourishes your mind and your heart.

It keeps your mind and your heart fit, strong and positive.

If you are constantly hearing the Word of God – and your mind is being
fed the Word of God on a daily basis – you are destined for success.

Romans 12:2 - I AM Carol Dixon!!!

ROMANS 12:2
*And be not conformed to this world: but be ye transformed
by the renewing of your mind, that ye may prove what [is]
that good, and acceptable, and perfect, will of God.*

"GOD HAS PROVIDED HEALING"

It is your covenant right to walk in divine health.

Some people say that God puts sickness and
disease on people to teach us something.

That is not in the Word! In fact, the opposite is true.

When multitudes of people came to Jesus, He had compassion on them
and healed them "all", not once did Jesus refuse to heal anybody.

God wants you to receive your healing.

He doesn't care whether you go to the physician or to the
minister as long as you put His Word first place in your life.

According to Proverbs 4 vs 22, the Word is health to your flesh.

Begin to put the Word in your heart, confess it,
and allow it to be medicine to your flesh.

Jesus Christ is the high priest of our confession,
and He will back His Word.

Your symptoms may tell you that you are sick,
but God says that you are healed.

Aren't you glad God doesn't want you sick?
Today, be thankful for God's provision for healing.

Matthew 14:14 -- I AM Carol Dixon!!!

MATTHEWS 14:14

*And Jesus went forth, and saw a great multitude, and was moved
with compassion toward them, and he healed their sick.*

"MOLDING YOUR THOUGHTS"

❦

You will never enjoy the kind of success that God says is yours if you can't see it in your mind and in your heart.

If you can mold it in your thoughts, then you will eventually hold it in your hands.

You have to be able to see it on the inside first.

In other words, outward prosperity comes in direct proportion to the prosperity of your soul.

Your soul is made up of your mind, your will, and your emotions.

When your mind is renewed to God's Word, your will is conformed to God's will, and your emotions are controlled by your reborn spirit: you will prosper.

Your greatest limitations are those in which you create in your mind by not casting down the thoughts that are contrary to God's Word.

Everything you experience outwardly is directly proportional to what you see and think of yourself inwardly.

3John 2 -- I AM Carol Dixon!!!

3 JOHN 2
Beloved, I wish above all things that thou mayest prosper and be in health, even as thy soul prospereth.

"PRESS TOWARD THE MARK"

❧✦❧

*O*ne of the most important success skills that you can develop is the ability to stay focused.

You can overcome any obstacle, any adversity that might come your way, when you are a focused believer.

Focus requires a target.

When you read God's Word and you discover God's promises for your life then that target has been created.

Here are four ways to stay focused: stay in the Word: God's Word builds you up.

When you stay in the word your faith remains strong.

Stay in faith: faith is what enables you to overcome the world.

Stay in fellowship: fellowship with the Holy Ghost puts you in a position of advantage.

And stay in joy: don't get so burdened down with believing that you lose your joy.

What is that "mark" you're pressing toward?

Whatever it is each day that you press, you're getting a little closer to it becoming reality.

Philippians 3:14 -- I AM Carol Dixon!!!

PHILIPPIANS 3:14
I press toward the mark for the prize of the high calling of God in Christ Jesus.

"IS ANYTHING TOO HARD FOR GOD?"

*I*t is vitally important that you realize there is an appointed time for the fulfillment of every promise of God, consequently, it eliminates a lot of frustration and when you are under the greatest pressure to give up, that's a good indication that your breakthrough is on the horizon.

God promised Abraham and Sarah that they would have a son, and you know the story: it was impossible.

Sarah's womb was dead and she's old.

That's two strikes against her.

Not to mention that her old man is old too.

That's three strikes.

But God says, "it shall come to pass at the appointed time." Why did God promise that?

Because nothing is too hard for God.

He's El Shaddai, when God promises something He has every intention of performing what He promised.

It never crosses His mind that it might not come to pass.

Don't let it cross yours.

Galatians 6:9 -- I AM Carol Dixon!!!

GALATIANS 6:9
And let us not be weary in well doing: for in due season we shall reap, if we faint not.

"NO LIMITS WITH GOD"

✦

*G*od gave us an example in the Old Testament of His ability to overcome circumstances by His miracle-working power.

He led two million people through the wilderness for forty years – though they complained loud and often about their plight.

There were no drug stores, no doctors, lawyers, housing units, or grocery stores, yet God took care of the Israelites and rewarded them.

He provided clothes and shoes that never wore out.

When they needed food, it rained down from heaven.

There are simply no limits with God!

God had repeatedly demonstrated His power to help us rise above the natural into the supernatural.

Are you or someone you love involved in a crisis right now?

I encourage you to look to Jesus today.

There are no limits with God.

Trust Him and He will reward you.

Hebrews 10:35 -- I AM Carol Dixon!!!

HEBREW 10:35

Cast not away therefore your confidence, which hath great recompence of reward.

"LET GOD TAKE CONTROL
OF YOUR LIFE"

❦

F irst Chronicles tells of a man by the name of Jabez, whose mother
so named him because she had difficulty delivering him.

His name means distress or sorrow or pain.

So Jabez had to go through life being constantly
reminded that he had caused pain and sorrow.

Maybe you have a bad name, not from the name your mother gave
you, but because of problems or troubles that have plagued you.

Do you know what Jabez did?

He prayed to the God of Israel to wonderfully bless
him and help him in his work and keep him from
evil disaster, and do you know what God did?

He granted his request.

It doesn't matter how bad your name is, when you turn to God
and look to Him as your Savior, He will grant you peace.

Let go of your past if it is troubling you, and
let God take control of your life.

1 Chronicles 4:10 – I AM Carol Dixon!!!

1 CHRONICLES 4:10
*And Jabez called on the God of Israel, saying, Oh that thou wouldest
bless me indeed, and enlarge my coast, and that thine hand might
be with me, and that thou wouldest keep [me] from evil, that it may
not grieve me! And God granted him that which he requested.*

"GOD IS DIRECTING YOUR STEPS"

꧁꧂

*I*f you trust in God with all your heart, He will direct your steps.

He purchased your salvation at Calvary, and as you allow
Him to be in charge of your life, you will become the
victorious Christian He intends for you to be.

When disasters come along that you don't understand – it
doesn't mean that God has stopped directing your steps.

He will just cause you to be able to handle it in the power of His Spirit.

You can rule and reign in life as a king.

He will cause all things to work together for
your good if you trust in Him.

Remember that regardless of your circumstances,
He is directing your paths.

Don't reason and try to understand everything.

Just let God give you strength, and you will be an overcomer.

You'll be more than a conqueror because He's directing your steps!

Proverbs 20:24 – I AM Carol Dixon!!!

PROVERBS 20:24
*Man's goings [are] of the LORD; how can a
man then understand his own way?*

"HE'S ALWAYS GOD"

⚜

*H*ow can God be described?
He is everything.

There is nothing that you can compare Him to because He is it.

He's all of it. He's always there. He is the great I am.
He is for us and never against us.

Whatever we need, He is there to provide for us.

He's merciful when we really don't deserve it.
He loves us because that's what He wants to do.

God is so full of compassion for His children that
He only wants us to have what's best for us.

And He's forgiving. He forgives our sins.

Isn't that wonderful and He not only forgives them, He forgets them!

We usually remember them, but He doesn't ever
bring them back to His remembrance.

God is also awesome, remarkable, and outstanding!
Just because He's God.

And I like Him just like He is – don't you?

Isaiah 40:18 - I AM Carol Dixon!!!

ISAIAH 40:18
*To whom then will ye liken God? or what
likeness will ye compare unto him?*

Carol Dixon   38   "60 Seconds"

"FEELINGS ...NOTHING MORE THAN FEELINGS"

In order to lay hold upon everything that God's Word promises you, you will have to put the Word of God ahead of your feelings and emotions.

Feelings and emotions will lie to you.

You're going to have to say, "nevertheless, at Thy Word." Do not allow yourself to be pulled into a different direction no matter how bad your situation, or how negative everyone around you may be.

Be focused, stay on the right path, yielding an ability to master every distraction, hence, getting you to that place that you truly want to go: you have to set aside time each day in the Word of God for fellowship with the Holy Spirit.

When you determine that your time with God is of utmost importance, and you refuse to allow anything or anyone to steal this time from you, then you will become a disciplined, focused believer and on your way to a victorious Christian life.

Romans 8:14 - I AM Carol Dixon!!!

Roman 8:14
For as many as are led by the Spirit of God, they are the sons of God.

"MAKE A CHOICE"

❧❦❧

*D*id you know that how you see yourself has everything to do with your destiny?

Your thoughts affect your outcome.

Your success is not dependent upon your circumstances.

In the eyes of God, your success is dependent upon how you see yourself.

If you think you're a failure, then you will fail.

If you think you can win through the power of God
that dwells within you, then you will win.

It's up to you. It's your choice. You can either believe
all the lies, or you can believe what God says.

Once you discover God's image and God's opinion, it's important that
you accept it, and then you'll be on your way to personal freedom.

The first thing that you need to know is this:
God does not create failures.

It's not His nature to fail; and it's not His will for you to fail.

If you can truly see yourself the way God sees you, then
every limitation will be removed from your life.

Proverbs 23:7 -- I AM Carol Dixon!!!

PROVERBS 23:7
*For as he thinketh in his heart, so [is] he: Eat and drink,
saith he to thee; but his heart [is] not with thee.*

"YOUR MAKEOVER"

❧❖❧

*T*he more you look into the Word, the more the image you have of yourself will change.

Another word for change is the word transformed; which means to change the shape and the appearance of.

God's Word is designed to paint a picture on the inside of you of the way God sees you.

The image that God has of you will cause you to be changed.

It's like a caterpillar becoming a butterfly.

Your self-image will go from feeling unworthy, shameful and inferior to realizing you are a unique, special, and a one-of-a-kind child of God!

You can't keep looking in the Word and see yourself failing-not when the Word says that you are more than a conqueror, that you're a world overcomer, and that you can do all things through Christ which strengthens you!

Begin to see yourself the way God sees you.

Get in His Word.

Realize that you are a unique, special child of God.

Psalms 139:14 – I AM Carol Dixon!!!

PSALMS 139:14
I will praise thee; for I am fearfully [and] wonderfully made: marvellous [are] thy works; and [that] my soul knoweth right well.

"THINK AHEAD"

※❖※

In order for you to enjoy a bright future, it is absolutely
necessary that you forget the past!

According to the Word, you are a new creation in
Christ Jesus and your past is forgiven.

Don't allow anything or anyone to destroy your life by
controlling your mind with thoughts about your past—
it's over, you are not that same person anymore.

Don't allow accusations that bring guilt into your life to keep you down.

Your mind will go into overtime with discouragement, feeling low
and so down on yourself that you will never be what God's called you
to be –but—the Word says: you are forgiven, you are accepted, you
are redeemed, you are chosen, you are predestined, you are blessed.

How in the world could you possibly lose if you
begin to see yourself the way God sees you?

Today is a new day and today God is doing a new thing in your life!

Isaiah 43:18 & 19 – I AM Carol Dixon!!!

ISAIAH 43: 18 & 19

18V Remember ye not the former things, neither consider the things of old.

*19V Behold, I will do a new thing; now it shall spring
forth; shall ye not know it? I will even make a way
in the wilderness, [and] rivers in the desert.*

"CONTROL YOUR THOUGHTS"

*D*o you control your thoughts you have about yourself
or do your thoughts control you?

Your attitude about yourself can either make you or break you.

It's time to start rejecting any thought that is contrary to God's Word.

Don't let your thoughts demoralize you.

Think on things that agree with what God says about you.

Many Christians do not have a revelation of who they are in Christ.

"For we are his workmanship, created in Christ Jesus…"
If you never learn to see yourself the way God sees you,
then your mind will be tormented with insecurities
which will ultimately affect every area of your life.

Make the Word final authority in your life.

When you do then you'll begin to walk in a greater level
of freedom than you've ever known in your life.

When you learn who you are in Christ, winning becomes
your way of life and losing becomes a thing of the past.

Ephesians 2:5 – I AM Carol Dixon!!!

EPHESIANS 2:5

*Even when we were dead in sins, hath quickened us
together with Christ, (by grace ye are saved ;)*

"FAITH VS. FEAR"

*ear and faith are both expectations; faith expects
the best and fear expects the worst.

What are you expecting?

Faith and fear are magnets: faith is a magnet that draws
provision and fear is a magnet that draws lack.

I want to encourage you to make the right choice today.

Don't let fear keep you from moving forward
in the plan of God for your life.

Fear is the opposite of faith. Fear and faith can not
co-exist; where you have one, you cannot have the other.

You receive from the enemy from fear, and you
receive from God through faith.

Choose to exhibit faith and boldness and start
enjoying the liberating freedom from fear.

Jesus overcame fear; He left it no power and no strength.

It has no-thing over you.

You need to choose-you only have one life to live, so live it
boldly and never let fear steal God's best from you.

2 Timothy 1:7---- I AM Carol Dixon!!!

2 TIMOTHY 1:7
*For God hath not given us the spirit of fear; but of
power, and of love, and of a sound mind.*

Carol Dixon   44   "60 Seconds"

"DON'T GIVE UP AND DON'T QUIT"

✻

*L*et me encourage you to not give up and to not quit.

It's time to pick yourself up, and declare that there is something great about to happen in your life.

No matter how devastating or overwhelming the attack might be right now, God can turn things around and cause the blessing to equally overwhelm you.

The blessing can wipe out everything, seriously!

The blessing is no respecter of persons.

The Bible says, "and all these blessings shall come on thee, and overtake thee... the Brenton translation says it like this: "all these blessings shall come upon you and shall find you..." the Hebrew says: "all these blessings shall reach you..." things are changing in your favor.

Your latter days will be better than your former days; I declare the rest of your life will be better than the first part of your life.

So choose to receive it by faith!

Deuteronomy 28:2--- I AM Carol Dixon!!!

DEUTERONOMY 28:2
"And all these blessings shall come on thee, and overtake thee, if thou shalt hearken unto the voice of the LORD thy God."

"RESTORE THE YEARS"

I am sure that God can make the rest of your life so rewarding and so fulfilling that it makes up for lost opportunities in your past.

God will restore the years that have been stolen from you.

Now, be honest, has the enemy stolen anything
from you over the last five years?

Do you want it back? Are you entitled to it? Yes, you are!

Let that sink in deep on the inside of you.

Start believing God for everything that has
been stolen from you sevenfold!

As a result, your lifestyle will change immediately.

Then you shall eat in plenty. Plenty is the nature of God.

That has been the plan for you and me since the beginning.

It never was the plan of God that you live in the land of "not enough" nor the land of "just enough", but God always intended for you and me to live in the land of "more than enough"!

Joel 2:25&26 --- I AM Carol Dixon!!!

JOEL 2:25&26

25v And I will restore to you the years that the locust hath eaten, the cankerworm, and the caterpillar, and the palmerworm, my great army which I sent among you.

26v And ye shall eat in plenty, and be satisfied, and praise the name of the LORD your God, that hath dealt wondrously with you: and my people shall never be ashamed.

Carol Dixon   46   "60 Seconds"

"REFUSE TO WASTE ANOTHER DAY"

༺✦༻

*T*here is a freedom and joy that comes from
living a proactive, purpose-filled life.

It's not always easy, but I'm praying that you will have the inner
strength to take the steps and conquer procrastination today!

Make up your mind that now is the time for you to do
those things you've been putting off—do it now.

What can you do today-even if it's five minutes-that will benefit you
tomorrow: pray in the spirit, read a Proverb, jump rope, empty the trash?

Do something each day that will lead you to fulfillment of your goals.

You will drastically change in just one month
by developing this daily discipline.

You'll begin thinking differently, your confidence will
improve, your faith in God will grow, your dreams will
enlarge, and your mind will be transformed!

Refuse to waste another day.

This is your time to see those dreams come to life.

James 2:17 --- I AM Carol Dixon!!!

JAMES 2:17
Even so faith, if it hath not works, is dead, being alone.

"DISCIPLINE"

⚜

L iving a disciplined life means that we practice
the Word of God on a consistent basis.

Getting up a little earlier, consistently every morning to read and
pray, takes discipline—but the reward is a closer relationship
with God and wisdom for making decisions in life.

Taking time to read your Bible every day may seem like a chore
at first, but the more you do it, the more revelation, the more
understanding and knowledge you will gain from God's Word.

If you will make a quality decision to live a life of discipline,
Jesus Christ Himself will help you follow through.

I encourage you to examine your life and think about
the blessing that may be blocked because you fail
to discipline yourself in the things of God.

When you realize what it is, decide today to change, because
the answer to your breakthrough just might be—discipline!

Philippians 4:13--- I AM Carol Dixon!!!

PHILIPPIANS 4:13
"I can do all things through Christ which strengtheneth me."

"GET THE TWO TOGETHER"

❧✦❧

"**E**stablished in the faith and abounding with thanksgiving."
These days it seems that's a rare combination.

A lot of people have been taught faith over the last several years, and
a lot of people have been taught to abound with thanksgiving.

But it's been hard to set the two together.

Faith folks want to confess the Word all the time,
but they don't praise God very much.

And those who like to praise God just want to jump and
shout and dance and have a good time in the Lord.

You can't get them to get very serious about the Word.

Success comes from combining the two – so do it!

Put them together in your life in the midst
of what's happening around you.

Keep thanking Him for the answer until it comes.

Instead of just standing on the Word, let the joy of the
Lord enable you to dance around on it a little.

It will get you where you're going a whole lot faster…and both
you and God will have a much better time on the way.

Colossians 2:1-10--- I AM Carol Dixon!!!

COLOSSIANS 2:1-10

1V "For I would that ye knew what great conflict I
have for you, and [for] them at Laodicea, and [for]
as many as have not seen my face in the flesh;"

2V "That their hearts might be comforted, being knit
together in love, and unto all riches of the full assurance
of understanding, to the acknowledgement of the mystery
of God, and of the Father, and of Christ;"

3V "In whom are hid all the treasures of wisdom and knowledge."

4V "And this I say, lest any man should beguile you with enticing words."

5v For though I be absent in the flesh, yet am I with
you in the spirit, joying and beholding your order,
and the stedfastness of your faith in Christ.

6v As ye have therefore received Christ Jesus the Lord, [so] walk ye in him:

7v Rooted and built up in him, and stablished in the faith, as ye
have been taught, abounding therein with thanksgiving.

8v Beware lest any man spoil you through philosophy
and vain deceit, after the tradition of men, after the
rudiments of the world, and not after Christ.

9v For in him dwelleth all the fulness of the Godhead bodily.

10v And ye are complete in him, which is the
head of all principality and power:

"STEP ACROSS THE FAITH LINE"

❧❖❧

A faith line is what you need when you want God to do the 'impossible' in your life.

It's what can make you like faithful Abraham, he had natural facts to deal with just like we do—there was no natural way for God's promise to him to come true.

Yet, Abraham ignored the natural evidence around him and believed only God's promise.

He made an irreversible decision to go with the Word of God.

So-how do you draw the faith line?

Begin with the Word.

Search the promises of God and purposely believe what He said, and is saying about your need.

Meditate on those promises until faith rises in your heart and mind.

From that moment on, speak only as if your miracle has already happened.

Turn your back on the problems, and doubts, and turn your face toward Jesus.

God will do the impossible in your life.

Dare to step across the faith line!

1Ttimothy 6:11&12---I AM Carol Dixon!!!

1 TIMOTHY 6:11&12

11V But thou, O man of God, flee these things; and follow after righteousness, godliness, faith, love, patience, meekness.

12V Fight the good fight of faith, lay hold on eternal life, whereunto thou art also called, and hast professed a good profession before many witnesses.

"PICK UP YOUR SWORD"

W hen you're up against the wall, don't start begging
God to break through it for you.

That's not the way He works.

He'll give you the plan. He'll give you the power.

And He'll guarantee the victory.

But your hand, not His own, is the instrument
He's going to use to get the job done.

You're going to have to stretch forth your hand by speaking and
acting on the Word even when circumstances are against you.

Just as God commanded His servant Moses, so Moses
commanded Joshua, and Joshua did it!

He didn't leave incomplete one thing that God had commanded Moses.

Joshua took the whole country.

Then he parceled out the land as an inheritance
to Israel according to their tribes.

And they had rest from war!

Don't wait for God to slay the dragon in your life.

You have the sword of the Spirit, the all powerful
Word of the living God, at your fingertips.

Pick it up and use it today---Joshua 11:5-23--- I AM Carol Dixon!!!

JOSHUA 11:5-23

5v And when all these kings were met together, they came and pitched together at the waters of Merom, to fight against Israel.

6v And the LORD said unto Joshua, Be not afraid because of them: for tomorrow about this time will I deliver them up all slain before Israel: Thou shalt though their horses, and burn their chariots with fire.

7v So Joshua came, and all the people of war with him, against them by the waters of Merom suddenly; and they fell upon them.

8v And the LORD delivered them into the hand of Israel, who smote them, and chased them unto great Zidon, and unto Misrephothmaim, and unto the valley of Mizpeh eastward; and they smote them, until they left them none remaining.

9v And Joshua did unto them as the LORD bade him: he houghed their horses and burnt their chariots with fire.

10v And Joshua at that time turned back, and took Hazor, and smote the king thereof with the sword: for Hazor beforetime was the head of all those kingdoms.

11v And they smote all the souls that [were] therein with the edge of the sword, utterly destroying [them]: there was not any left to breathe: and he burnt Hazor with fire.

12v And all the cities of those kings, and all the kings of them, did Joshua take, and smote them with the edge of the sword, [and] he utterly destroyed them, as Moses the servant of the LORD commanded.

13v But [as for] the cities that stood still in their strength, Israel burned none of them, save Hazor only; [that] did Joshua burn.

14v And all the spoil of these cities, and the cattle, the children of Israel took for a prey unto themselves; but every man they smote with the edge of the sword, until they had destroyed them, neither left they any to breathe.

15v As the LORD commanded Moses his servant, so did Moses command Joshua, and so did Joshua; he left nothing undone of all that the LORD commanded Moses.

16v So Joshua took all that land, the hills, and all the south country, and all the land of Goshen, and the valley, and the plain, and the mountain of Israel, and the valley of the same;

17V [Even] from the mount Halak, that goeth up to Seir, even unto Baalgad in the valley of Lebanon under Mount Hermon: and all their kings he took, and smote them, and slew them.

18v Joshua made war a long time with all those kings.

19v There was not a city that made peace with the children of Israel, save the Hivites the inhabitants of Gibeon: all [other] they took in battle.

20v For it was of the LORD to harden their hearts, that they should come against Israel in battle, that he might destroy them utterly, [and] that they might have no favour, but that he might destroy them, as the LORD commanded Moses.

21v And at that time came Joshua, and cut off the Anakims from the mountains, from Hebron, from Debir, from Anab, and from all the mountains of Judah, and from all the mountains of Israel: Joshua destroyed them utterly with their cities.

22v There was none of the Anakims left in the land of the children of Israel: only in Gaza, in Gath, and in Ashdod, there remained.

23v So Joshua took the whole land, according to all that the LORD said unto Moses; and Joshua gave it for an inheritance unto Israel according to their divisions by their tribes. And the land rested from war.

"CREATED TO PRAISE"

&

*W*e're created to praise God.

According to the Bible, if you breathe, you were meant to praise.

When you first begin to truly praise, it may seem awkward to you, but if you'll keep it up, it will become a way of life.

Why?

Because praise causes the Glory of God to manifest in your life. It causes you to walk in the light of His countenance.

It will start a revival inside of you!

And don't just think of praising Him in the congregation. Praise Him in your own private time and throughout your day.

Learn to maintain an attitude of praise and thanksgiving.

When praise becomes natural to you in your own private life, it won't be difficult to praise Him in the midst of the congregation.

Are you longing for a revival of God's presence in your life?

Are you tired of just hearing about the glorious manifestations of His power in the past?

Then open your mouth and your heart and do what God has created you to do—praise!

Psalms 150:6 --- I AM Carol Dixon!!!

PSALMS 150:6
"Let everything that hath breath praise the LORD. Praise ye the LORD."

"LET THE WORLD KNOW"

※❖❖

*O*ver the years the church has come up with all kinds
of elaborate ways to evangelize the world.

Most believers don't even realize that he gave
us the key to winning the world.

He prayed about it right before he went to the cross.

He asked the Father to bring us into a place of such
oneness with each other and with Him that the world
would know that He had been sent from God.

Do you want to take a step toward evangelizing the world today?

Then start praying for oneness.

Make up your mind that you're going to
start loving your fellow believers.

Start confessing that the church of God is going to rise up together in
faith and love as one glorious body driven by the power of Jesus Himself.

Jesus prayed that it would happen, and the Holy
Spirit is already bringing it to pass.

It's going to let the whole world know that Jesus truly is Lord!

John 17:20, 22 and 23--- I AM Carol Dixon!!!

JOHN 17: 20, 22, 23

*20v "Neither pray I for these alone, but for them also
which shall believe on me through their word;"*

*22v "And the glory which Thou gavest me I have given
them; that they may be one, even as we are one:"*

Carol Dixon   57   "60 Seconds"

23v *"I in them, and thou in me, that they may be made perfect in one; and that the world may know that thou hast sent me, and has loved them, as Thou hast loved me."*

"YOU ARE RIGHTEOUS"

I don't care how badly you may have messed things up yesterday or how many mistakes you have made.

I want you to begin this day knowing you are righteous!

Not because of anything you've done but because you've received, by faith in Jesus, the righteousness of God.

Here are some benefits the word of God says that righteousness will bring:

"The righteous shall flourish like the palm tree" (Ps. 92:12)

"The seed of the righteous shall be delivered" (Prov. 11:21)

"For the eyes of the lord are over the righteous, and his ears are open unto their prayers" (1Peter 3:12)

"I have been young, and now I am old; yet have I not seen the righteous forsaken, nor his seed begging bread" (Ps. 37:25)

Don't be robbed of these blessings by feeling unworthy, shake it off! Shout out loud, "I am the righteousness of God"!

Then step out in faith and enjoy the privileges God has prepared for you! Romans 3:21-28--- I AM Carol Dixon!!!

ROMANS 3:21-28

21v "But now the righteousness of God without the law is manifested, being witnessed by the law and the prophets;"

22v "Even the righteousness of God [which is] by faith of Jesus Christ unto all and upon all them that believe: for there is no difference:

23v For all have sinned, and come short of the glory of God;

24v "Being justified freely by his grace through the
redemption that is in Christ Jesus:"

25v Whom God hath set forth [to be] a propitiation through
faith in his blood, to declare his righteousness for the remission
of sins that are past, through the forbearance of God;

26v To declare, [I say], at this time his righteousness: that he might
be just, and the justifier of him which believeth in Jesus.

27v Where [is] boasting then? It is excluded. By what
law? of works? Nay: but by the law of faith.

28v Therefore we conclude that a man is justified
by faith without the deeds of the law.

"LOVE IS THE POWER CHARGE"

Love is the first and foremost command Jesus gave us,
yet all too many believers neglect to follow it.

Do you want to see the incredible power of
God released through your life?

Then start putting the love command in action.
Faith works by love.

In fact, none of the Gifts of the Spirit will work if you don't have love.
Love is the power charge.

God's power package just won't work without it.

That's why we've seen so many power failures in the body of Christ.

Starting today, you and I can turn those failures around.

We can make up our mind to let the Word dwell richly within us.

We can set our hearts on keeping the commands of Jesus
and speak His name with confidence and authority.

And, most important of all, we can begin to love one another.

Then we will truly see the power of God begin to flow.

John 15:12 & 13--- I AM Carol Dixon!!!

JOHN 15:12&13

*12v "This is my commandment, That ye love
one another, as I have loved you."*

*13v "Greater love hath no man than this, that a
man lay down his life for his friends."*

Carol Dixon   61   "60 Seconds"

"A HIDDEN TREASURE"

Right now, at this very moment, you have hidden within you a treasure that can change the world.

A treasure that can turn a person's poverty into prosperity, sickness into health, sorrow into joy.

You have within you the all powerful God.

Sow it into the hearts of those you meet. Share it at every opportunity. "But I don't know how!" You may say.

Then start learning.

Let these three steps help guide the way: make a decision that you are going to share the Word with others no matter what!

Commit to it.

Once you've done that, you'll find the rest is easy.

Then, prepare yourself by meditating in the Word each day. Allow the Holy Spirit to minister to you. That will make it easy for you to minister to others.

Finally, stay in faith, and trust God for the results.

The Word of God does not return void.

What are you going to do with your hidden treasure today?

Mark 4:14---I AM Carol Dixon!!!

MARK 4:14
"The sower soweth the Word."

Carol Dixon   62   "60 Seconds"

"JOY: A VERY REAL FORCE"

·❦·

*J*oy.
It's not a warm, happy feeling you're supposed to have
now and then when things are going well.

It's much more than that.
Joy is one of the most powerful spiritual forces in the world.

You can't live a life of faith without being strong in the Lord-and when
God wants to make you strong; joy is what he uses to do the job!

Joy is a very real force, just as fear has to yield to
faith; discouragement has to yield to joy.

Since joy is one of the fruits of the Holy Spirit,
you already have it residing within you.

But you must develop it, confess it, and live
by it if you want to enjoy its power.

Whatever circumstances you are facing today, you can be full of joy.
You can be strong in the Lord.

You can draw on the supply of the Holy Spirit in you and come out on top.

So rejoice-rejoice!

Nehemiah 8:10---I AM Carol Dixon!!!

NEHEMIAH 8:10
*"Then he said unto them, Go your way, eat the fat, and drink
the sweet, and send portions unto them for whom nothing
is prepared: for [this] day [is] holy unto our Lord: neither
be ye sorry; for the joy of the LORD is your strength."*

Carol Dixon   63   "60 Seconds"

"PUT THE WORD FIRST"

❧❧❧

*G*od has been raising up ever growing numbers
of people who are hungry.

Hungry to know their Lord in a deeper way.

Hungry to serve Him-in pulpits, on mission fields, in homes, in
office buildings, and anywhere else He might choose to send them.

Are you among them, if so, I want to share four simple words that
will enable you to run the race like a winner: put the Word first.

Whether your goal is to be an excellent evangelist or a first
rate engineer in the service of the Lord it is the wisdom that
comes from the Word of God that will get you there.

So commit yourself right now to do whatever it takes to
totally saturate yourself with the Word of God.

Read, study, listen to, and meditate on it.

Be diligent and put the Word first and there
will surely be glorious victories ahead.

Proverbs 4:5&6--- I AM Carol Dixon!!!

PROVERBS 4:5 & 6

*5v "Get wisdom, get understanding: forget [it] not;
neither decline from the words of my mouth."*

*6v "Forsake her not, and she shall preserve thee:
love her, and she shall keep thee.*

"YOU CAN OPEN THAT DOOR"

***

Some people spend years trying to work their way out of financial binds only to end up more bound by debt.

Others work doggedly on marriages that, despite their best efforts, deteriorate from year to year.

Still others fight battles against fear or depression, drug addiction or disease.

Each of you know there must be an answer to the problems you face—but often it seems to be hidden behind a door that's locked tightly against you.

What I want you to know today is this: you can open that door!

Jesus Himself has given you the keys. God's Word is full of keys.

There's no situation so dark and so cleverly designed by the forces of darkness that there is not a kingdom key that will unlock it with kingdom power.

There is an answer to your situation.

If you've been digging in the Word of God in one spot and haven't found your answer, keep digging until you find the key.

Keep knocking until you find the door that opens.

Matthew 7:7--- I AM Carol Dixon!!!

MATTHEW 7:7
"Ask, and it shall be given you; seek and ye shall find; knock, and it shall be opened unto you:"

"CALLED TO INTERCESSION"

There's a desperate need for believers who are willing to be intercessors.

Those who will go before God and reach out for His mercy and compassion for the sinner, for the sick, and for this downcast world.

For prayer warriors who will stick with it until they have the assurance inside, in their spirits, that every barrier is broken and every area of bondage has been abolished.

There are certain things that won't happen on this earth until He finds them.

There are blessings and moves of God that won't come until someone gives birth to those things by prayer.

Even the Lord Jesus Himself was ushered into the earth by intercession.

Remember Simeon and Anna?

They prayed for the Messiah to come-but when they were done, they saw Jesus as a tiny baby in the temple, they recognized Him and rejoiced.

Someone needs you to pray them through – spend some time on your knees today.

Matthew 5:4---I AM Carol Dixon!!!

MATTHEW 5:4
"Blessed [are] they that mourn: for they shall be comforted."

"PEACE AT HOME"

❧❈❧

*H*ave you ever noticed that the easiest place
to remain self-centered is at home?

There's an incentive to be lovely with others, but with
your family you are tempted to allow yourself more
selfish privileges as if it didn't count there.

If you are more courteous and nicer to friends than to your family-
--that's got to change, if you are more demanding and less forgiving
with those dearest to you than with anyone else---that must change!

Make Jesus Lord of your life and begin to learn through the
Word of God the importance of harmony within your family.

Learn that if you want the power of agreement to work
in your lives, you cannot allow strife in your home.

Strife drops the shield of faith; it stops prayer results,
and invites all kinds of evil work into your midst.

It also paralyzes the power of God in your life.

Put the power of harmony to work in your family today!

James 3:16---I AM Carol Dixon!!!

JAMES 3:16
*"For where envying and strife [is], there [is]
confusion and every evil work."*

"THE CHOICE IS YOURS"

✠

Choosing to side with God's Word is a continual challenge.

It's a process of choosing to believe and act upon the
Word of God over and over in every circumstance.

That's what everyone has to do.

Years ago I decided I was going to choose Jesus.

Since then I've had to choose Him again
and again in situations every day.

I've chosen Him as my Lord and Savior.

I've chosen Him as my healer. I've chosen Him as my financier.
I've chosen Him as head of my ministry.

And I still have to choose Him moment by moment.

Sometimes the choice gets tough, but God
promised it will never get too tough.

He said He will not allow you to be subjected to
a temptation you're unable to overcome.

With every temptation, He'll make a way of escape.

He'll always make sure you have a choice.

So choose to walk in love, to walk by faith,
to live by the Word – choose Him!

Joshua 24:15--- I AM Carol Dixon!!!

JOSHUA 24:15

"And if it seem evil unto you to serve the LORD, choose you this day whom ye will serve; whether the gods which your fathers served that [were] on the other side of the flood, or the gods of the Amorites, in whose land ye dwell: but as for me and my house, we will serve the LORD."

"DON'T STOP AT THE GATE"

❧✽❧

When you made Jesus the Lord of your life, one of the privileges you received was the right to come to the throne room of God any time you want to.

Think about that!

You have the right to go boldly before God and obtain whatever you need.

Even though that's clearly what the Bible says, many people don't go boldly into the throne.

Instead they think, "I could never go into where God is—I'll just stand out here and yell and hope He hears me".

As you are begging and pleading, bombarding the gates of heaven for revival-the Lord is speaking- "what are you doing, those gates are not locked.

Why don't you quit bombarding them and just come on in?" Do you need to receive something from God today?

Don't waste time standing around outside heaven's gates.

Through Jesus you belong in the very throne room of God. So come right on in and obtain mercy and grace.

The door is always open for you.

Hebrews 4:16--- I AM Carol Dixon!!!

HEBREWS 4:16
"Let us therefore come boldly unto the throne of grace, that we may obtain mercy, and find grace to help in time of need."

"BEYOND WHAT YOU CAN ASK OR THINK"

~*~

*P*raying in tongues is the only way you and
I can pray beyond what we know.

It's the tool God has given us to use to tap into the mind of the Spirit.

As a result, the Holy Spirit within us begins to teach us and enlighten us.

Apostle Paul is an example, he said he prayed in tongues
more than anyone in the whole Corinthian church, and he
was responsible for writing most of the New Testament.

Another example is the first church at Jerusalem.

They prayed in tongues until the revelation
light of God dawned in their hearts.

That's all the equipment they had.

So they used it and turned the world upside down.

If you haven't made a commitment to spend some time
each day praying in tongues, make one now.

God has plans for you that are so good your human mind hasn't even
conceived them-things that are beyond what you can ask or think.

Tap into the mind of God.

Pray in the Spirit today.

1 Corinthians 14:18--- I AM Carol Dixon!!!

1 CORINTHIANS 14:18
"I thank my God, I speak with tongues more than ye all:"

Carol Dixon   71   "60 Seconds"

"TITHE WITH JOY"

***

Most Christians aren't very excited about tithing.

But they should be and they would be if they
understood how to do it properly.

Scriptural tithing stirs up faith.

It activates the power of God in our lives when we do it in
gratitude and joy, expecting our needs to be met abundantly.

God has brought us out of a life of bondage and poverty
into a life that flows with the abundance of God.

So when you bring your tithe to the Lord,
follow the example of the Israelites.

Make it a time of rejoicing.

Make it a time of realizing anew the wonderful
things Jesus Christ has done for you.

Thank Him for bringing you into his promised
land of mercy, joy, peace, and prosperity.

Tithe in faith, expecting the rich blessings of
that land to be multiplied to you.

You may soon find it to be one of the most
exciting things you can do.

Deuteronomy 26:1 & 2 --- I AM Carol Dixon!!!

DEUTERONOMY 26: 1 & 2

*1v "And it shall be, when thou [art] come in unto the
land which the LORD thy God giveth thee [for] an
inheritance, and possessest it, and dwellest therein;"*

*2v "That thou shalt take of the first of the fruit of the earth, which
thou shalt bring of thy land that the LORD thy God giveth thee,
and shalt put [it] in a basket, and shalt go unto the place which
the LORD thy God shall choose to place his name there."*

"GUARANTEED SUCCESS IN THE KINGDOM OF GOD"

*H*ow bad do you want to succeed in life?

Most people want to experience success in their endeavors but they are really unsure of how to achieve the success they desire.

According to the world's system, success is achieved by how hard you work, whether you have the right connections and whether or not you are willing to compromise at times.

But God's formula for success is different.

It is determined by three things: 1) keeping the Word of God in your mouth, 2) meditating on it and 3) acting out on what God says.

When you follow his three-part formula for success, you can't fail.

Success in the world's system comes with a price tag of misery, but the blessing of God will make you rich and has no sorrow attached to it.

The Holy Spirit will save you time, money and energy when you stay vitally connected to God and his Word.

Once you put God's formula for success into operation, you will begin to see the breakthrough you've been believing God for.

Joshua 1:5---I AM Carol Dixon!!!

JOSHUA 1:5
"There shall not any man be able to stand before thee all the days of thy life: as I was with Moses, [so] I will be with thee: I will not fail thee, nor forsake thee."

"SPIRITUAL FARMING"

❧❖❧

*T*he same principles farmers use to yield a bountiful harvest of
vegetables or fruit are the same ones that believers are
supposed to use to experience the harvest of
God's blessings in their lives.

Any farmer must first put seed in the ground
before he can harvest his crop.

Then, there is a waiting period in which he must be patient.

During that time, he must watch over his crop to make sure it is
properly watered and cared for, making sure that his field or garden
is protected from animals or pests that may try to eat his goods!

God's system of operation is identical to natural farming
in that it also operates by seedtime and harvest.

Christians are the spiritual 'farmers' who must diligently
plant seeds and exert effort to harvest their blessings.

It won't be long before your seed grows up into a mighty harvest
that will bless you and all those who cross your path!

Mark 4: 26- 27--- I AM Carol Dixon!!!

MARK 4: 26 & 27

*26v "And he said, So is the kingdom of God, as if a
man should cast seed into the ground;"*

*27v "And should sleep, and rise night and day, and the seed
should spring and grow up, he knoweth not how."*

"DON'T SETTLE FOR SECOND BEST"

If you'll use your trials to develop patience, you're going to be totally supplied in every way, in want of nothing.

Patience doesn't mean settling sweetly for the second best.

No, patience is a powerful word.

The New Testament meaning of it, as translated literally from Greek, is 'to be consistently constant or to be the same way all the time, regardless of what happens.' To understand how much power is involved in that, you have to realize it's one of the most outstanding attributes of God Himself.

The Bible says He's the same yesterday, today and forever.

God has that much power!

And by the power of the Holy Ghost working within you, you can be the same everyday no matter what happens.

If you'll put your trust in the Word of God and let patience go to work, it won't matter what happens.

You won't ever have to accept anything less than victory again.

James 1:2 & 3--- I AM Carol Dixon!!!

JAMES 1:2 & 3

2v "My Brethren, count it all joy when ye fall into divers temptations;"

3v "Knowing [this], that the trying of your faith worketh patience."

"DEVELOPING A HUNGER FOR GOD"

Are you dissatisfied on the inside?

Do you feel like your spiritual walk has dried up?

I have good news for you today!

"Hold on to what you have learned-remind yourself of it!"
You need to constantly be refreshed in the scriptures.

I want to challenge you to stir yourself up and
continue in what you have learned.

God is using every form of communication and media to get
revelation into your life, but sometimes you try to live off of what
you've heard instead of it continually being refreshed in you.

God responds to hunger.

If you are waiting on God to do this or that—He is waiting
for you to get desperate for His power and His Spirit to
move—hungry and thirsty again to see His glory.

When that happens, you will be filled!

Don't live on yesterday's food.

Continually feed your spirit with the Word of God!

Matthew 5:6--- I AM Carol Dixon!!!

MATTHEW 5:6
*"Blessed [are] they which do hunger and thirst after
righteousness: for they shall be filled."*

"TURN YOUR EAR TOWARD HEAVEN"

⊱✦⊰

*E*very moment of every single day you're listening
to someone, you're hearing many voices.

But, if you're a believer you have another voice speaking to you as well.

It's the voice of the Holy Spirit.

He has the solutions to every situation you will encounter.

However, you have to hear Him and believe His report.

The voices of fear are speaking loudly, but you
must refuse to be moved by them.

I'm not saying to pretend that a problem doesn't exist.

What I am saying is to use your faith to attack
the problem, with the Word of God.

No voice on earth has a greater impact on
your circumstances than your own.

Your outcome will be based on the Words of your mouth.

So let me ask: what voices are you listening to?

Turn your ear toward heaven, the Spirit is speaking.
Get in agreement with what the Spirit is saying.

Proverbs 8:34 — I AM Carol Dixon!!!

Proverbs 8:34
*"Blessed [is] the man that heareth me, watching daily
at my gates, waiting at the posts of my doors."*

Carol Dixon   78   "60 Seconds"

"YOU'RE SOMEBODY SPECIAL TO GOD"

※❖※

"**Y**ou're so special to God—you are his treasure!

He considers you the most valuable of all his creations.

God has crowned you with glory and honor!

You are God's prized possession.

You are more important than all his handiwork".

You need to see yourself in that light.

If you are born again, the very divine nature of God is within you and the blood of Jesus flows through your veins.

You are of a royal family in the spirit realm.

You have a crown on you that can't be seen with the natural eye, but you can walk in that honor because you are highly favored by God.

When you truly believe that you will take authority over every adverse circumstance in you life and expect God to turn your adversity into victory.

Receive God's love for you and see yourself as His prized treasure---because you are!

John 3:16--- I AM Carol Dixon!!!

JOHN 3:16
"For God so loved the world, that he gave his only begotten Son, that whosoever believeth in him should not perish, but have everlasting life."

"KNOWING GOD"

"**M**any of God's people are struggling, some are giving up and turning away." But for those who will remain faithful and be determined to know their God, the best is yet to come.

God wants to pour out His blessing.

However, you must be in position to receive them.

There is a place in God where it becomes joyful to trust Him, but you have to get to know Him, then you can understand this.

When your motivation for studying the Bible is so that you can know Him, not becoming selfish, self-centered, and only wanting what He will give you, then you will discover that your relationship will put you in position to have your every need met.

I want to challenge you to study the Word of God intimately.

He wants to reveal Himself to you.

Then it becomes a joy to trust Him and the struggle is over!

Ephesians 3:10--- I AM Carol Dixon!!!

EPHESIANS 3:10
"To the intent that now unto the principalities and powers in heavenly [places] might be known by the church the manifold wisdom of God,"

"FAITH FOR TODAY"

I learned many years ago that faith is the victory that overcomes the world (1 John 5:4), and it will continue to be the victory, no matter what is going on in the world.

For that reason we must continue to develop our faith and never allow anything or anyone to talk us out of it.

Living by faith is a lifestyle.

Be careful about what you subject yourself to.

God has imparted truth into your spirit, and you can't let thieves come along and steal it.

As you are diligent in the Word, there will be a built-in "security alarm" that goes off when you hear things that aren't true.

What brings freedom?

Truth.

You only know the truth when you continue in the Word. Freedom is an ongoing process-so continue in the Word!

Don't be moved by what you see or what you hear, but be moved by God's Word!

John 8:31 & 32--- I AM Carol Dixon!!!

JOHN 8: 31 & 32
31v "Then said Jesus to those Jews which believed on him, If ye continue in my word, [then] are ye my disciples indeed;"

32v "And ye shall know the truth, and the truth shall make you free."

Carol Dixon   81   "60 Seconds"

"NO TURNING BACK"

❧❀❧

I have found that it is easy to see where Christians really are with the Lord when times of pressure and persecution come.

I want to encourage you today to make the
decision that there is no turning back!

Everything you desire is ahead of you, not behind you.

The closer you get to the appearance of Jesus, the more
intense the attacks in your life will become.

At the same time, if you have your eyes on Jesus and your heart
full of God's Word, then you won't grow weaker and weaker as
the attacks intensify, but you will grow stronger and stronger!

Major attacks will bring major victories!

I want to encourage you to put your hand to the plow.

Make up your mind that you are going to go
forward, no matter what comes against you.

Then at the end of the day you will be able to say, "I have fought
a good fight, I have finished my course, I have kept the faith".

2 Timothy 4:7--- I AM Carol Dixon!!!

2 TIMOTHY 4:7
*"I have fought a good fight I have finished [my]
course, I have kept the faith:"*

"EXTRAORDINARY"

***

I am expecting God's best this year.

Let me share with you a word that God gave
me, I heard the Spirit of God say this:

"Beginning in 2012, I will do for you what you've
tried to do yourself but could not do.

I will cause to come to pass those things which you've strived
for and tried to accomplish in your own strength and in
your own might but just could not make it happen.

I will bring them to pass for you.

Extraordinary things will become the norm in your life.

Things that never happened to most people in a
lifetime will happen to you in one year's time"!

I believe that is a Word from God for all of us.

When God makes statements like this, we need to realize that
it's time for us to stretch our faith, stretch our imaginations,
and think bigger than we've ever thought before.

Begin to look for the extraordinary to become the norm in your life!

Habakkuk 1:5--- I AM Carol Dixon!!!

HABAKKUK 1:5

*"Behold ye among the heathen, and regard, and wonder
marvelously: for [I] will work a work in your days,
[which] ye will not believe, though it be told [you]."*

"A NEW THING"

✦❖✦

God wants us to begin to expect the extraordinary. Forget about the past and don't limit God.

You haven't seen everything God can do, but if you will dare to believe, then you will!

God is doing a new thing.
And if God wants to do a new thing, then let him do it!

He says in Isaiah, "I will work, and who can hinder or reverse it?" God is going to do this and it cannot be stopped.

Governments are not going to be able to stop it.
The economy won't be able to stop it.

It's going to happen and you can either expect it to come to pass in your life or just hear about it happening to others.

Either way, it's going to happen.

It's a new thing-this is the beginning of the extraordinary, the remarkable, and the rare.

Today start confessing that you are not normal.

You are living in the realm of the extraordinary!

Isaiah 43:18 & 19--- I AM Carol Dixon!!!

ISAIAH 43:18 & 19

18v Remember ye not the former things, neither consider the things of old."

19v "Behold, I will do a new thing; now it shall spring forth; shall ye not know it? I will even make a way in the wilderness, [and] rivers in the desert."

"EXTRAORDINARY MIRACLES"

~✦~

$\mathcal{P}$aul always experienced miracles in his ministry.

But in Acts he entered into a new thing that had
not been happening to him before.

Acts 19 in the Amplified Bible says: "and God did unusual
and extraordinary miracles by the hands of Paul." Something
began to happen in Paul's life that was not the norm.

Clothing that touched his body was put on other
people who were sick or demon possessed.

And whenever those pieces of cloth were placed upon people.

They were made whole and delivered.

I would call that extraordinary!

Paul always experienced miracles in his ministry.

But then he entered into a new thing that had
not been happening to him before.

God is saying, "the way I performed the miracles you've seen
in the past is not the only way I can perform them.

I'm going to show you new ways in the days ahead."
Acts 19: 11 & 12 --- I AM Carol Dixon!!!

ACTS 19: 11 & 12

11v "And God wrought special miracles by the hands of Paul:"

*12v "So that from his body were brought unto the sick
handkerchiefs or aprons, and the diseases departed from
them, and the evil spirits went out of them."*

"BECOME WHAT YOU BELIEVE"

When the blind men asked Jesus to restore their sight, he asked them if they believed He could perform the miracle that they had asked for, and they said, "Yea, Lord." It goes on to say, "then touched He their eyes, saying, according to your faith be it unto you.

And their eyes were opened." Those who believe He is able to do it will receive miracles.

The message translation says it this way: "Jesus said to them, do you really believe I can do this?

They said, why, yes, Master!

He touched their eyes and said, become what you believe." You are today what you believed about yourself yesterday.

And, tomorrow you will be what you believe about yourself today.

Do you like how you are today?

Do you like how your life is?

If not, then change what you believe about yourself and what you believe about your life—become what you believe.

Matthew 9:29 – I AM Carol Dixon!!!

MATTHEW 9:29

" *Then touched he their eyes, saying, According to your faith be it unto you.*"

"WHERE ARE YOUR WORDS TAKING YOU"

Speaking wrong words is like crossing electric wires.

You cause things to happen that you don't want to happen.

But when you speak right words, you release the
power of God to operate in your life.

Let me ask you, what have you been saying lately?

You hold the power to change your life through the words you speak.

Through your words, you are building a road over
which you will travel to your destiny.

If you speak negatively and contrary to the Word of God, that
road will take you away from what God has promised you.

But if you continually speak in line with the Word, your
highway will lead to an abundant life filled with peace,
prosperity, health, deliverance, and every other blessing.

Your talk always precedes your walk.

So make up your mind to speak only words of life---words
that will bring the good things of God to you---words
that will pave the road to your God-given destiny.

Proverbs 18:21 --- I AM Carol Dixon!!!

PROVERBS 18:21
*"Death and life [are] in the power of the tongue: and
they that love it shall eat the fruit thereof."*

"WORDS FITLY SPOKEN"

Whenever you speak God's Word, you release the power of God to operate in your life.

One thing is certain: whatever you are saying today is what you will get in the future.

Some people never obtain what God has planned for them because they aren't speaking the right words.

And whether you like it or not, you are living in line with what you are saying.

Your mouth should be filled with what the Word of God says.

You should be saying things like, "God always gives me the victory through my Lord Jesus Christ" (1Cor. 15:57) "I always triumph in Christ" (2 Cor. 2:14).

"I always have more than enough money to meet all of my needs and to sow generously into the kingdom of God" (2 Cor. 9:8).

"No illness can prevail in my life because the stripes of Jesus have healed me from all sickness and disease" (1 Peter 2:24).

When you talk like this, your life and personal situations will turn around.

So speak God's Word, and release the power of God to operate in your life.

Proverbs 6:2 --- I AM Carol Dixon!!!

PROVERBS 6:2
"Thou art snared with the words of thy mouth, thou art taken with the words of thy mouth."

Carol Dixon 88 *"60 Seconds"*

"CREATE YOUR WORLD"

❧✦❧

You can create and frame your world through your words.

Your daily confession will build a highway toward a bright future.

Say this confession with me: "my future is in my words.

I will walk in God's bright future for me by speaking the right words.

I'm calling those things that do not exist as though they do.

I maintain a constant confession of faith, I obey God's Word, and I will see what God has promised in His Word come to pass in my life.

Instead of sickness, I have health.

Instead of poverty, I have wealth.

I declare the Word, and I live in line with it, thereby, nothing but the good comes unto me"---when you talk like this, your life and personal circumstances will turn!

Hebrews 11:3 --- I AM Carol Dixon!!!

HEBREWS 11:3
"Through faith we understand that the worlds were framed by the word of God, so that things which are seen were not made of things which do appear."

"*WORD*"

Every day you speak countless words, often paying very little attention to the words themselves.

I would like you to reflect on the kind of words you have been speaking.

Are they negative words or positive words?

Are they uplifting words or harsh words?

Perhaps you need to put a watch over your lips.

You need to be careful of the words you speak to your spouse, children and loved ones.

Your words can either hurt or heal.

They can inspire or destroy.

Too many times, you speak harshly to your family.

Make it a practice to only allow faith-building, positive words to come forth from your mouth.

So, don't wring your hands in despair, you have your turn around in your mouth---make your bold declaration of harvest, and let God take it from there!

Philippians 4:13 --- I AM Carol Dixon!!!

PHILIPPIANS 4:13
"I can do all things through Christ which strengtheneth me."

"YOUR MOST POWERFUL WEAPON"

I fondly remember the story I read as a child about the train that fought its way up a steep hill, saying, "I think I can, I think I can." As the "little engine that could" was about to accomplish his mission, he began to exclaim, "I know I can, I know I can." You need to take that same attitude whenever adverse circumstances come your way.

Your head-your thoughts-may give you a problem.

Your head will scream in your ears, "you're going to fail this time!

You're going under this time!

You're not going to make it this time"!

When your mind is being fiercely attacked, that is when you must allow the written Word of God to flow forth from your mouth.

Don't ever face the attacks with your mouth shut!

Your mouth is your most powerful weapon!

Boldly declare, "none of these things move me"!

Acts 20:24 --- I AM Carol Dixon!!!

ACTS 20:24
"But none of these things move me, neither count I my life dear unto myself, so that I might finish my course with joy, and the ministry, which I have received of the Lord Jesus, to testify the gospel of the grace of God."

"REJOICE"

❧❦❧

Don't allow test and trials of life to keep you from rejoicing!

Jesus himself said, "In this world ye shall have tribulation,
but be of good cheer; I have overcome the world"!

We are to delight ourselves in God and His Word
and not fret over our circumstances.

We are to rejoice in God's goodness, mercy, and abounding grace.

We can rejoice in our unchanging God and
that His Word does not change!

When you encounter troubles, tests, and trials,
remember this: you're just passing through!

Don't pitch camp on the problems.

Just keep on walking, rejoicing in the God of your salvation!

David said he was walking through!

Pass through the valley of tests and trials, rejoicing in God.

His Word says, there's a blessing coming with your name on it.

Psalm 67:6 --- I AM Carol Dixon!!!

PSALM 67:6
*"[Then] shall the earth yield her increase; [and]
God, [even] our own God, shall bless us."*

"A SEED KNOWS"

❧❀❧

*L*et's talk about seeds today.

Our whole world operates on the law of seedtime and harvest.

So seeds are important.

A seed only knows how to do one thing---produce a harvest.

A seed will do its best to grow when it's planted.

Even if you throw it out in the middle of the
highway, it will do its best to spring up.

It may not be in the right soil, but it will do its
best, because that's all it knows to do.

I have had hard times when I have given to people and never
asked for a return on my seed, but God blessed me anyway.

The DNA of a seed is increase and multiplication.

If you will be mindful of this spiritual law and put God first.

If you show him that He's first place in your life, then things
are going to begin to be added to your life like never before.

Genesis 8:22 --- I AM Carol Dixon!!!

GENESIS 8:22
*"While the earth remaineth, seedtime and harvest, and cold and heat,
and summer and winter, and day and night shall not cease."*

"FEARLESS CONFIDENCE"

One of the best ways to keep your expectations high is to remember that God promises to reward your faith.

Sometimes people are afraid to raise their expectations because they don't want to be disappointed if God doesn't come through.

But I don't know the God who doesn't come through, I know the God who does.

I have heard people say, "don't get your hopes up too high.

You never know what God might do." Well, God is a God of integrity.

I have discovered that God does exactly what he says he'll do in His Word.

I don't know how He'll do it.

But I do know that He will do what His Word says He will.

The Bible says that you will not be disappointed.

You're going to get exactly what you expect.

If you will not give up, God will come through for you.

God will reward your faith.

Proverbs 23: 17 & 18 --- I AM Carol Dixon!!!

PROVERBS 23: 17 & 18

17v "Let not thine heart envy sinners: but [be thou] in the fear of the LORD all the day long."

18v "For surely there is an end; and thine expectation shall not be cut off."

Carol Dixon   94   "60 Seconds"

"QUESTIONS"

For the extraordinary to become the norm in your life, all God is commanding you to do is simply believe.

Your question should never be "can God" or "will God"?

It is never a question about God's ability.

He is able to do whatever needs to be done for you.

The question you need to be asking yourself is: "How do I get in position to receive---to receive the extraordinary"?

To answer this question you need to understand that every seed produces after its own kind.

If you want the extraordinary in your life, then you have to plant extraordinary seeds.

You're going to have to do more now than what you have done in the past.

Get out of the norm and get into the extraordinary.

Mark 5:36 --- I AM Carol Dixon!!!

MARK 5:36
"As soon as Jesus heard the word that was spoken, he saith unto the ruler of the synagogue, Be not afraid, only believe."

"HIGHER THOUGHTS"

❧❀❧

God wants to enlarge your capacity to receive
by enlarging your thinking.

If you think small, you will stay small.

Your ability to receive is directly linked to your ability to comprehend.

Don't limit God any longer.

Renew your mind in the Word of God and
you will not think in terms of lack.

You will think plenty, abundance, and more than enough.

The more God's Word penetrates your heart and renews
your mind, the greater your possibilities become.

You become focused-you get up, when you're knocked down.

Even when you have setbacks, you keep pressing forward!

A single thought that you allow to drop into your
spirit and meditate upon can change your entire
destiny…what you think is what you become.

Become the winner God has predestined for you to be.

Proverbs 21:5 --I AM Carol Dixon!!!

PROVERBS 21:5
*"The thoughts of the diligent [tend] only to plenteousness;
but of every one [that is] hasty only to want."*

ACKNOWLEDGEMENTS

My ongoing gratitude to my Publishing family at Westbow Press.

I'm indebted to Tasha, Yvonne, and Barbara for helping
me take this much - needed message to the next level.

To Bonquita, Jenine, DeJuan, LaShira, Brittany and Wesley,
you all amaze me more every day with your unconditional
love and enthusiastic spirit – I am grateful…

Thank You

"These Inspirational Minutes are
heard daily on the radio".

❧❀❧

Please feel free to contact me through my website at
www.caroldixon.org
or write to me at
P.O. Box 24831, Detroit, MI, 48224.

I hope "60 SECONDS" has been a blessing to you. I pray
that God will use the thoughts He has provoked through
the Inspirational Minutes to strategically orchestrate
miraculous progress through all the days of your life…

Taking you from Glory to Glory!!!